CORDOBA TRAVEL GUIDE 2024

The Complete Guide to Cordoba Beautiful Sights, History, Food, and Culture. All the information you need to know before traveling to Cordoba

By Paula Robertson

copyright© 2023 Paula Robertson

All rights are reserved. No part of this publication may be copied, distributed, or communicated in any form or by any means, including photocopying, recording, or other electronic or mechanical methods, without the prior written consent of the publisher.

INTRODUCTION	**6**
Overview of Cordoba	6
Cordoba's History	8
When to Go to Cordoba	10
CHAPTER 1: GETTING TO CORDOBA	**13**
Transportation Alternatives	13
How to Get Around in the City	14
CHAPTER 3: WHERE TO STAY	**17**
Accommodation Types	17
1st Class Hotels	17
Low-Cost Alternatives	17
Exceptional Boutique Hotels	17
Vacation Rentals and Airbnb	18
Historic Inns & Guesthouses	18
Paradores	18
Eco-Friendly Places to Stay	18
Long-Term Stays	18
Luxury Hotels	19
Budget-Friendly Alternatives	21
Boutique Hotels that are One-of-a-Kind	22
CHAPTER 4: EXPLORING CORDOBA	**25**
Top Attractions in Cordoba	25
Galleries and Museums	27
Green Spaces and Parks	29

CHAPTER 5: DINING AND FOOD — 33

- CORDOBAN CUISINE MUST-TRY DISHES — 33
- RESTAURANTS AND CAFES IN THE NEIGHBORHOOD — 35
- CORDOBA VEGETARIAN AND VEGAN OPTIONS — 37
- CORDOBA DINING ETIQUETTE — 39

CHAPTER 6: NIGHTLIFE & ENTERTAINMENT — 43

- PUBS AND BARS — 43
- CORDOBA LIVE MUSIC AND CONCERTS — 45
- CORDOBA'S THEATER AND PERFORMING ARTS — 47
- CORDOBA NIGHTCLUBS AND DANCING — 49

CHAPTER 7: CORDOBA SHOPPING — 53

- SOUVENIRS AND PRESENTS — 53
- CORDOBA'S TRADITIONAL MARKETS — 55
- CORDOBA'S HIGH-END BOUTIQUES — 57
- CORDOBA'S SHOPPING DISTRICTS — 60

CHAPTER 8: DAY TRIPS & EXCURSIONS — 63

- AZARA MEDINA — 63
- CORDOBA SIERRA — 64
- MONTILLA-MORILES WINE TOURS — 65
- CARMONA EXCURSION — 67
- SURROUNDING VILLAGES OF CORDOBA — 68

CHAPTER 9: USEFUL INFORMATION — 71

- COMMUNICATION AND LANGUAGE — 71

TRANSPORT	72
PAYMENT AND CURRENCY	72
REGIONAL CUSTOMS	73
SAFETY RECOMMENDATIONS	73
MEDICAL AND HEALTH SERVICES	75

CHAPTER 10: TRIP PLANNING 77

SUGGESTIONS FOR ITINERARIES	77
ONE-DAY ITINERARY: CORDOBA HIGHLIGHTS	77
ITINERARY FOR TWO DAYS: DEEPER EXPLORATION	78
ITINERARY FOR THREE DAYS: LEISURELY EXPLORATION	79
PACKING SUGGESTIONS FOR A TRIP TO CORDOBA	80
BUDGETING AND COSTS FOR YOUR CORDOBA TRIP	83

CONCLUSION 87

INTRODUCTION

Overview of cordoba

Cordoba is a historic and charming city in southern Spain recognized for its rich history, beautiful architecture, and dynamic culture. Cordoba, located in the geographic center of Andalusia, maintains a distinctive place in the country's legacy and is a must-see destination for visitors looking for a mix of history, art, and real Spanish experiences.

Historical Importance

Cordoba has a rich history that dates back thousands of years. It was a major Roman city before turning into the capital of the Islamic Caliphate in the eighth century, rivaling towns such as Baghdad and Constantinople in terms of cultural and intellectual impact.

Architectural Wonders

The city is famous for its spectacular Mezquita, also known as the Cordoba Mosque-Cathedral, which is a UNESCO World Heritage site. This architectural marvel features a beautiful fusion of Islamic and Christian design elements.

Charm of an Old Town

The "Juderia, " or historic old town, of Cordoba is a maze of small alleyways, whitewashed buildings, and lovely courtyards filled with colorful flowers. It's a lovely spot to meander around and take in the ambience.

Cultural Blending

Cordoba is a living example of many civilizations coexisting throughout history. You may discover its unique tapestry of influences through its cuisine, music, and festivals, which combine Moorish, Christian, and Jewish traditions.

Celebrations and Festivals

The city comes alive during numerous events, the most well-known of which is the Patio Festival, in which residents offer their magnificently decorated courtyards to the public. Semana Santa (Holy Week) and Feria de Cordoba, a colorful fair full with dance, music, and wonderful cuisine, are also celebrated in Cordoba.

Gastronomy

Cordoba's culinary scene is exquisite, with delicacies such as salmorejo (cold tomato soup), flamenqun (fried ham and cheese buns), and the famed Cordoban-style rabo de toro (oxtail stew). Dining in classic pubs and attractive eateries is an experience in and of itself.

Natural radiance

The city is surrounded by beautiful scenery, such as the Sierra de Cordoba mountain range and the Guadalquivir River. Hiking, motorcycling, and birdwatching are just a few of the outdoor activities available at these natural treasures.

Pleasant Hospitality

Cordoba is noted for its kind people. The sincere kindness of the inhabitants typically embraces visitors, making their stay even more unforgettable.

Location that is easily accessible

Cordoba's center location in Andalusia makes it a great starting point for seeing the region's other notable cities, including Seville, Granada, and Malaga.

Cordoba is a place that promises an extraordinary voyage through time and culture in the heart of Spain.

Cordoba's history

Cordoba, located in southern Spain, has a rich history dating back over two millennia. Here's a quick rundown of Cordoba's history:

Cordoba in the Acient Times

Cordoba's history may be traced back to pre-Roman periods, when it was inhabited by numerous Iberian tribes. In the second century BCE, it became an important Roman metropolis known as "Corduba" and served as the capital of the Roman province of Hispania Ulterior Baetica.

Cordoba developed as a center for culture, administration, and olive oil manufacturing throughout Roman authority.

Golden Age of Islam

The Umayyad Caliphate took Cordoba in the eighth century, ushering in the Islamic era in Al-Andalus (Islamic Spain).

Cordoba had a cultural and intellectual rebirth after becoming the capital of the Islamic Caliphate in the early eighth century. During this time, the Great Mosque of Cordoba (Mezquita) was completed, displaying superb Islamic architecture. Cordoba was recognized as a center of study and scholarship, with academics such as Averroes and Maimonides making significant contributions to numerous subjects.

It was a varied city, with Muslims, Christians, and Jews coexisting and adding to its cosmopolitan flavor.

Reconquest of Christianity

During the Reconquista, a series of operations to reclaim Spain from Islamic dominion, Christian soldiers took Cordoba in the 13th century.

The Mezquita was turned into a Christian cathedral to represent the changing religious environment of the city. During this time, Gothic and Renaissance architecture, such as the Alcázar de los Reyes Cristianos, were popular in Cordoba.

Jewish ancestry

During the Islamic era, Cordoba's Jewish community thrived, contributing to the city's cultural and intellectual life. With its tiny alleyways and antique synagogues, the Jewish Quarter (Juderia) is a testimony to this heritage.

Modern Period

Over the years, Cordoba evolved as a Spanish metropolis while keeping its historical and cultural history.

Cordoba is currently recognized for its exciting festivities, including as the Patio Festival and Semana Santa, delectable cuisine, and architectural marvels such as the Mezquita-Cathedral.

Cordoba's history is a fascinating voyage through time, reflecting the influences of numerous civilizations and leaving behind a great cultural legacy that enchants people from all over the world.

When to Go to Cordoba

The best time to visit Cordoba, Spain, depends on your weather, event, and crowd preferences. Cordoba has four distinct seasons, each of which offers a distinctive experience. Here's a summary of the seasons and when they're best to visit:

From March until May: One of the most popular periods to visit Cordoba is in the spring. With temperatures ranging from 15°C to 25°C (59°F to 77°F), the weather is pleasant.

The city's famous Patio Festival is held in early May, when the courtyards of Cordoba are in full bloom, giving it an ideal opportunity to observe this beautiful spectacle.

Spring is also perfect for visiting historic places and enjoying outdoor activities without the sweltering heat of summer.

Summer months (June to August): Summer in Cordoba may be quite hot, with temperatures frequently above 30°C (86°F) and occasionally exceeding 40°C (over 100°F).

Summer, despite the heat, attracts a large number of tourists, particularly in June and July. If you can stand the heat, you may enjoy the city's lively atmosphere and outdoor events. During the summer, it's critical to stay hydrated and protect yourself from the sun.

September until November (Autumn): Autumn is also a great time to explore Cordoba. The weather begins to cool down after a hot summer, with temperatures ranging from 18°C to 28°C (64°F to 82°F) in September and steadily decreasing. When opposed to the summer months, the city is less busy, making it simpler to explore its attractions and enjoy its restaurants and cafes.

From December until February (Winter): Cordoba's winters are mild, with daily temperatures ranging from 12°C to 18°C (54°F to 64°F). This is the off-season for tourists, so expect less people and reduced hotel fees.

Winter can be a wonderful season to come if you don't mind the cooler weather and prefer a more peaceful atmosphere. Some outdoor attractions, however, may have reduced hours or be closed for renovation.

To summarize, the optimal time to visit Cordoba is determined largely by your tolerance for heat and choice for people. Spring and fall are the most pleasant and popular seasons, with agreeable weather and stimulating cultural activities. Summer might be a fun season to visit the city if you can tolerate the heat. Winters are more tranquil, although you may need to be flexible with your plan owing to closures.

CHAPTER 1: GETTING TO CORDOBA

Transportation Alternatives

When planning a vacation to Cordoba, take into account the many transportation alternatives accessible to get to this charming city in southern Spain. Cordoba is well-connected to major Spanish cities and has a variety of handy ways to get there.

By Air

Cordoba Airport (Aeropuerto de Córdoba): While there is an airport in Cordoba, it mostly services domestic flights and may not be the most convenient alternative for international visitors. It is, nonetheless, advantageous for people flying in from other Spanish cities.

Seville Airport (Aeropuerto de Sevilla): Located around 130 kilometers (81 miles) from Cordoba, Seville's international airport serves as a significant gateway to the region. Many foreign planes land here, and Cordoba is easily accessible by train or bus from Seville.

Malaga Airport (Aeropuerto de Málaga-Costa del Sol): Another option for foreign passengers is Malaga's international airport, which is roughly 160 kilometers (99 miles) from Cordoba. Cordoba, like Seville, may be reached by train or bus from Malaga.

Taking the Train

High-Speed AVE Trains: The high-speed AVE train network connects Cordoba to other major Spanish cities. The trip from Madrid to Cordoba takes about 1. 5 to 2 hours, making it a practical option for visitors from the capital. Cordoba is additionally connected by AVE trains to Seville, Malaga, and Barcelona.

Regional Trains: Regional trains are available for touring other parts of Andalusia or neighboring regions. They offer a more comfortable and cost-effective way to visit Cordoba.

By Bus

Bus Services: Several bus companies provide trips to Cordoba from cities throughout Spain. Cordoba's bus station is conveniently placed in the city center, giving it a good option for travelers who prefer ground transportation.

By Car

Road Trips: Consider renting a car if you want freedom and want to see the Spanish countryside. Major highways connect Cordoba, and travelling through the lovely Andalusian landscapes can be a wonderful experience.

Parking: Because parking in the old city center might be difficult, it's best to check with your hotel about parking choices or use public parking facilities.

Transportation by Public

Local Buses: Once you arrive in Cordoba, you can use the city's excellent local bus network to move around. For convenience, you can buy tickets on the bus or get a reloadable transportation card.

You can organize your trip to Cordoba with ease if you understand the transportation alternatives available, assuring a smooth and delightful visit to this historical and cultural gem in Spain.

How to Get Around in the City

You'll want to visit Cordoba and its many attractions once you arrive. Cordoba is a very small city with a variety of transit alternatives to assist you get around. Here's a map of the city to help you navigate around:

1. Strolling

Exploring the Historic Center: The historic center of Cordoba is best explored on foot. The Jewish Quarter (Juderia), lovely courtyards, and several historical sites are all within walking distance of one another.

Scenic stroll: Take leisurely stroll along the Guadalquivir River, see the Roman Bridge, and meander through the lovely Alcazar gardens.

2. Two bicycles

Bike Rentals: Bike rentals are available in Cordoba, making it simple to explore the city on two wheels. You can rent bicycles for a few hours or for the entire day.

Bike Routes: The city boasts designated bike lanes and trails that allow you to explore Cordoba's attractions while taking in the scenery.

3. Public Transport

City Buses: Cordoba has a well-developed bus system that serves the entire city. You can buy tickets on the bus or use a reloadable transit card for convenience.

4. Taxis

Taxi Services: Taxis can be found throughout Cordoba. They are an efficient means of transportation for getting to certain locations rapidly.

5. Tourist Train

Cordoba Tourist Train: The city has a tourist train that takes you on a guided tour of the city's major sights. It's a fun and instructive way to see the city.

6. Rental Automobiles

Renting a Car: If you want to explore locations outside of the city, such as the Andalusian countryside or nearby towns and villages, renting a car can be a convenient option. Keep in mind, however, that parking in the historic district can be limited.

7. Carriages Drawn by Horses

Carriage Rides: A horse-drawn carriage ride through Cordoba's old neighborhoods is a unique and romantic experience. It's a nice way to see the beauties of the city.

8. Walking Tours

Guided Walking Tours: Participating in a guided walking tour lead by a skilled local guide can provide insights into Cordoba's history and culture while exploring its landmarks.

Cordoba's small size and well-preserved historic core make it perfect for exploring on foot or by bike. For longer excursions or convenience, public transportation and taxi services are also easily available. Regardless of your mode of transportation, you'll find that Cordoba is a simple city to explore, allowing you to fully immerse yourself in its rich history and lively culture.

Chapter 3: Where to Stay

When organizing a trip to Cordoba, it's critical to select lodging that meets your interests and needs. Cordoba has a variety of hotel alternatives, each offering a unique experience. In this chapter, we'll look at the many sorts of lodging accessible in the city.

Accommodation Types

Cordoba has a wide range of lodging alternatives to suit all preferences and budgets. Here are some examples of where to stay in the city:

1st Class Hotels

Cordoba has several 5-star and boutique hotels noted for their excellent service, gorgeous accommodations, and remarkable amenities. Some of these hotels are built in historic structures and provide a unique blend of modern comfort and classic charm.

Low-Cost Alternatives

Hostels & Guesthouses: Cordoba boasts a number of budget-friendly hostels and guesthouses that offer reasonable and clean lodging for budget-conscious guests. These are fantastic choices for backpackers and single travelers.

Exceptional Boutique Hotels

Historic Riads and Boutique Hotels: Consider staying in a boutique hotel or riad for a more intimate and culturally rich experience. Many of these properties are housed in ancient structures, providing a window into Cordoba's past.

Vacation Rentals and Airbnb

Apartments and holiday Homes: Apartments and holiday homes in Cordoba can be found on Airbnb and other vacation rental services. This choice is ideal for tourists looking for a home-like experience with plenty of space and facilities.

Historic Inns & Guesthouses

Pensiones and Posadas: Traditional inns and guesthouses known as "pensiones" and "posadas" may be found in Cordoba, and these quaint and typically family-run accommodations offer an authentic Spanish experience.

Paradores

Paradores: Paradores are a network of unique and historic hotels located in important cultural and historical places around Spain. Cordoba has its own parador, which provides a luxurious stay in a historically significant environment.

Eco-Friendly Places to Stay

Eco-Lodges: If you're concerned about the environment, you may locate eco-friendly lodging in and around Cordoba. These options promote environmental responsibility and sustainability.

Long-Term Stays

Long-Term Rentals: If you intend to stay in Cordoba for an extended amount of time, you can look at long-term rental choices including furnished apartments and serviced apartments, which offer additional space and services for longer stays.

Consider variables like as location, budget, amenities, and the type of experience you seek when booking your accommodation in Cordoba. The city's varied choice of housing options guarantees that there is something to suit any traveler, whether they are looking for luxury, history, or a more affordable stay.

Luxury Hotels

Cordoba has a variety of magnificent hotels that offer unrivaled comfort, exquisite facilities, and a sense of opulence. Staying in one of these luxury hotels might take your Cordoba experience to the next level. Here are some of the city's notable luxury hotels:

1. Hospes Palacio del Bailio Hotel

This 5-star luxury hotel is set in a stunningly renovated 16th-century palace. It combines ancient charm with contemporary elegance.

The hotel has a beautiful courtyard with a pool, a spa, and a gourmet restaurant serving Andalusian cuisine. Conveniently placed in the historic center, near key sights such as the Mezquita-Cathedral.

2. Hotel Eurostars Palace

This contemporary 5-star hotel on the Guadalquivir River offers elegant and stylish accommodations. Amenities include a panoramic outdoor pool, a fitness facility, and a restaurant serving both local and international cuisine.

The Mezquita-Cathedral and other historical monuments are within walking distance.

3. Amistad Cordoba by NH Collection

A four-star hotel housed in two 18th-century mansions, offering a unique blend of historical architecture and modern luxury. A garden, a terrace, a restaurant, and spacious, well-appointed rooms are available to guests.

Location: Located in the heart of the Jewish Quarter, this hotel provides an excellent starting point for visiting Cordoba's historic center.

4. Cordoba Balcon Hotel

This boutique hotel is noted for its cozy environment and attractive Andalusian decor. The hotel has a rooftop terrace with beautiful views, a traditional Andalusian patio, and a charming courtyard.

Location: In the heart of the Jewish Quarter, near the Mezquita-Cathedral.

5. Cordoba's Houses of Judaism

A one-of-a-kind 4-star hotel made up of interconnecting old dwellings that form a labyrinthine structure. The hotel has various courtyards, swimming pools, and a spa. Every room has a unique charm of its own.

Location: In the center of the Jewish Quarter, close to the city's main attractions.

Staying in one of Cordoba's luxury hotels not only guarantees a comfortable and opulent stay, but it also frequently immerses you in the city's rich history and architectural legacy. These hotels are well-located, allowing you to discover Cordoba's cultural riches while also enjoying the best in hospitality and services.

Budget-Friendly Alternatives

Travelers looking for low-cost accommodations in Cordoba have various possibilities. Cordoba has inexpensive lodging options that provide comfort and convenience without breaking the wallet. Here are some low-cost alternatives:

1. Guesthouses and Hostels

Hostal La Fuente: This strategically located hostel provides clean and pleasant rooms at reasonable prices. It's a good alternative for budget-conscious vacationers and backpackers.

Hostal Osio: Located in the historic center, Hostal Osio offers inexpensive rooms in a traditional Andalusian setting. It is near notable sites such as the Mezquita-Cathedral.

2. Hotels on a Shoestring

Hotel Selu: A three-star budget hotel with comfortable rooms, a restaurant, and a central position near the city center.

Hotel Don Paula: Located within walking distance of Cordoba's attractions, this budget-friendly hotel offers simple but adequate lodgings.

3. Pensiones and Posadas in Cordoba

Pensiones: There are various pensiones (pensions) in Cordoba that offer inexpensive rooms. These are frequently family-owned and provide a warm, welcoming atmosphere.

Posadas: Posadas are modest inns or guesthouses that are reasonably priced. They provide a comfortable atmosphere and are an excellent choice for budget guests.

4. Camping and hostels located outside of the city

Camping Las Camachas: This camping park, located just outside of Cordoba, provides economical options for guests with tents or campers. It's a tranquil option for individuals who appreciate nature.

Youth Hostels: There are also youth hostels located outside of the city center, which provide a cost-effective choice for those who are willing to go a little further to the city's attractions.

5. Vacation Rentals and Airbnb

Apartments: Airbnb has a selection of low-cost apartments and holiday rentals in Cordoba. This option provides a home-like environment and frequently includes kitchen facilities.

It's critical to evaluate your tastes, travel style, and goals when looking for low-cost lodging. While these options may have fewer amenities than luxury hotels, they allow you to save money on lodging, giving you more money to discover Cordoba's historical and cultural treasures. Cordoba has possibilities for every budget-conscious visitor, whether you prefer hostels, guesthouses, budget hotels, or unique local experiences like pensiones and posadas.

Boutique Hotels that are one-of-a-kind

Boutique hotels in Cordoba provide a wonderful blend of customized service, unique ambiance, and often historical significance for guests seeking a more intimate and culturally diverse experience. These establishments are noted for their attention to detail and unique personality. Here are several one-of-a-kind boutique hotels in Cordoba:

1. Viento Hotel10

Hotel Viento10, located in a magnificently renovated 17th-century mansion, offers a quiet ambience and stylish décor. The motel is a modest boutique with a nice courtyard.

The hotel's amenities include pleasant rooms, a terrace with city views, and a library. The crew is well-known for its hospitality.

Location: Located in the historic core of Cordoba, near the Mezquita-Cathedral and other attractions.

2. Córdoba Balcony

This boutique hotel is housed in a 17th-century townhouse that has been meticulously refurbished to preserve its historical charm. It is well-known for its Andalusian architecture and welcoming atmosphere.

The Balcón de Córdoba has a beautiful patio, a rooftop terrace, and elegantly appointed rooms. The on-site restaurant serves regional fare.

Location: Located in Cordoba's Jewish Quarter, this hotel provides easy access to the city's historic sights.

3. The Azulejos' House

Casa de los Azulejos is a one-of-a-kind boutique hotel notable for its beautiful blue and white tilework (azulejos). It is housed in a historic structure with Moorish characteristics.

Rooms are attractively designed, and it is a central courtyard and a rooftop terrace with views of the Mezquita-Cathedral.

The hotel is located in the centre of the historic district, near to the main attractions.

4. Cordoba's Houses of Judaism

This boutique hotel is made up of interconnected old houses, resulting in a labyrinthine pattern reminiscent of Cordoba's history.

Guests can enjoy several courtyards, swimming pools, and individually decorated suites. Each space has its own distinct personality and charm.

Location: Authentic and immersive experience in the Jewish Quarter.

5. Conde de la Palma's Palace

Casa Palacio Conde de la Palma, a boutique hotel built in a 16th-century palace, offers an elegant and historic ambiance.

The hotel's amenities include pleasant rooms, a courtyard with a fountain, and a lounge area. It is renowned for having a calm atmosphere.

Location: The hotel is centrally placed, making it convenient to go around Cordoba and see the sights.

Staying at a one-of-a-kind boutique hotel in Cordoba allows you to immerse yourself in the city's history and culture while also enjoying customized service and distinctive surroundings. These establishments frequently represent Cordoba's architectural and artistic legacy, making your stay unique and authentic.

Whether you choose Airbnb or another vacation rental company, these alternatives give a home-away-from-home experience in Cordoba, allowing you to explore the city at your own leisure while also enjoying the conveniences of a private apartment.

Chapter 4: Exploring Cordoba

Cordoba is a city rich in history and culture, with a plethora of sights and experiences to offer visitors. In this chapter, we'll look at some of Cordoba's top attractions and must-see locations that highlight the city's rich history.

Top Attractions in Cordoba

Cordoba is rich in historical, architectural, and cultural riches. Here are some of the must-see sights in Cordoba:

1. Mezquita-Cathedral (Cordoba's Great Mosque)

The Mezquita-Cathedral is Cordoba's most recognizable feature and a UNESCO World Heritage Site. It is a magnificent architectural masterpiece that depicts the city's varied past.

Highlights include the enthralling forest of horseshoe arches, the mihrab (prayer niche), the Patio de los Naranjos (Orange Tree Courtyard), and the Christian altar erected after the Reconquista.

2. Alcázar de los Reyes Cristianos (Christian Monarchs' Alcazar)

After the Reconquista, this historic castle and stronghold served as a residence for Christian rulers. It has lovely gardens, courtyards, and amazing architecture.

Highlights include a stroll around the gardens, a visit to the royal baths, and a climb to the top of the tower for panoramic views of Cordoba.

3. Juderia (Jewish Quarter)

The Jewish Quarter is a charming and historic neighborhood known for its tiny lanes, whitewashed buildings, and strong Jewish heritage.

Highlights include the Synagogue (one of the oldest in Spain), the Casa de Sefarad (Sephardic House), and the Juderia's beautiful lanes.

4. Puente Romano (Roman Bridge)

The Roman Bridge is a reminder of Cordoba's historic heritage. It crosses the Guadalquivir River and provides spectacular views of the Mezquita-Cathedral.

Highlights includesTaking a stroll across the bridge, especially at night when it is beautifully illuminated.

5. Torre de la Calahorra (Calahorra Tower)

This antique tower was formerly used as a defensive fortification. It is presently home to the Museum of Al-Andalus Life, which celebrates the city's Islamic past.

Highlights: Explore the museum's displays and gaze out the tower's window at the Mezquita-Cathedral.

6. Patio Festival (Fiesta de los Patios) on June 6th

Don't miss the Patio Festival in May, a UNESCO-recognized event in which people open their courtyards to display exquisite flower arrangements and decor.

Highlights: Take a stroll around the courtyards decked with bright flowers and soak in the charm of Cordoba's patios.

7. Azahara Medina

Medina Azahara, located just outside of Cordoba, is a remarkable archaeological site that showcases the remnants of a large medieval imperial city.

Highlights: Explore the unearthed remnants and acquire insights into Al-Andalus' rich lifestyle at its peak.

These are just a few of the many attractions available in Cordoba. The rich history, architectural wonders, and dynamic culture of the city offer several chances for exploration and discovery.

Galleries and museums

Cordoba is not only rich in architectural beauties, but also in museums and galleries that provide insights into the city's history, culture, and art. Here are some of the city's notable museums and galleries to visit:

1. Al-Andalus Life Museum (Museo Vivo de Al-Andalus)

This museum, housed in the Calahorra Tower, focuses on Cordoba's Islamic origins and the Al-Andalus period.

Highlights of Al-Andalus include exhibits on daily life, art, science, and technology. In addition, the museum has interactive displays and immersive experiences.

2. Córdoba Museum of Fine Arts (Museo de Bellas Artes)

This museum, located in the historic center, displays a collection of Spanish paintings and sculptures from the Middle Ages to the twentieth century.

Highlights include works by well-known Spanish artists such as Francisco de Zurbarán, Bartolomé Esteban Murillo, and Luis de Morales.

3. Cordoba's Archaeological and Ethnological Museum (Museo Arqueológico y Etnológico de Córdoba)

This museum honors Cordoba's archaeological legacy and ethnological collections, displaying artifacts dating from prehistoric times to the present.

Highlights include archaeological artifacts, antique pottery, Roman mosaics, and ethnographic exhibits depicting regional daily life.

4. Sefarad House (Sephardic House)

Casa de Sefarad is a cultural center and museum honoring Sephardic Jewish ancestry. It focuses on the history, culture, and contributions of Cordoba's Sephardic Jews.

Highlights include a visit to the beautifully renovated building, which hosts exhibitions, workshops, and cultural events centered on Jewish history and traditions.

5. Cordoba Botanical Garden (Jardn Botánico de Córdoba)

This botanical park, located near the Alcazar, displays a diverse range of plant species from throughout the world.

Highlights: Take a tranquil stroll through themed gardens such as the Mediterranean, tropical, and aquatic gardens.

6. Julio Romero de Torres

This museum honors the life and works of Julio Romero de Torres, a well-known Cordoban painter noted for his portraits and portrayals of Cordoba.

Highlights: View a gallery of his works and read about the artist's impact on the cultural scene in Cordoba.

7. Popular Arts and Customs Museum (Museo de Artes y Costumbres Populares)

This museum, housed in a historic structure, exhibits traditional Andalusian crafts, costumes, and everyday artifacts.

Highlights include exhibits on area cultures, festivals, and local craftsmen' work.

Cordoba's museums and galleries provide a wide range of experiences, from learning about the city's Islamic history to enjoying its creative heritage. Cordoba's museums and galleries contain something for everyone, whether they are interested in history, art, or culture.

Green Spaces and Parks

While famed for its historical and architectural wonders, Cordoba also has calm parks and green places where visitors may relax, appreciate nature, and take leisurely strolls. Here are various parks and green spaces to visit in the city:

1. Alcázar de los Reyes Cristianos Gardens (Alcazar Gardens)

The gardens around the Alcazar are a tranquil haven of lush foliage, fountains, and beautiful pools.

Highlights: Explore the various portions of the gardens, such as the Cypress Courtyard and the Moorish-style garden with orange trees. Don't miss the Alcazar's calm environment and wonderful views.

2. Cordoba Botanical Garden (Jardn Botánico de Córdoba)

This botanical park, located near the Alcazar, houses a diverse collection of plant species from throughout the world.

Highlights include strolling through themed gardens such as the Mediterranean, subtropical, and aquatic sections. The garden is a peaceful haven for nature enthusiasts and photographers.

3. Asomadilla National Park

This park is a local favorite for outdoor activities and leisure. It has parks, playgrounds, and walking pathways.

Highlights: Have a picnic, go for a jog, or simply enjoy the fresh air in a peaceful setting. The park is popular with locals and families.

4. Cruz Conde Park

Parque Cruz Conde is one of Cordoba's largest parks, notable for its wide areas, tree-lined streets, and recreational facilities.

Highlights: Take a stroll through the park's gardens, play spaces, and sports courts.

5. Miraflores Park

Parque de Miraflores, located along the Guadalquivir River, provides spectacular river views as well as a comfortable location for outdoor sports.

Highlights: Take a walk or cycling along the riverbanks, relax in the shady places, and enjoy the scenery. The park is great for a peaceful afternoon.

6. Sotos de la Albolafia Park

This park, named after the Albolafia waterwheel, offers a scenic riverbank setting with green spaces and trails.

Highlights: Take a relaxing walk along the river, take in the shade of the trees, and see the views of the Mezquita-Cathedral and the Roman Bridge.

7. The Victoria Park

The Parque de la Victoria is a well-kept park with planted gardens, sculptures, and recreational areas.

Highlights: Take in the peaceful environment of the park, appreciate the sculptures, and spend quality time with friends or family.

Cordoba's parks and green areas offer a welcome respite from the city's hustle and bustle, allowing you to unwind, connect with nature, or simply take a leisurely stroll. Whether you want to visit botanical gardens, riverside parks, or local favorites, these green spaces provide a unique viewpoint on Cordoba's beauty and charm.

Chapter 5: Dining and Food

Cordoba is well-known not just for its historical and architectural beauties, but also for its thriving gastronomic scene. In this chapter, we'll look at the peculiar Cordoban cuisine and where you may sample the city's delectable specialties.

Cordoban Cuisine Must-Try Dishes

Cordoban cuisine reflects the region's rich history, incorporating elements from its Roman, Moorish, Jewish, and Christian ancestors. The cuisine of the region is recognized for its use of fresh ingredients, simple yet tasty dishes, and a concentration on traditional recipes handed down through generations. The following are some significant components of Cordoban cuisine:

1. Salmorejo: Salmorejo is a cold tomato and bread soup that is thicker and creamier than gazpacho. It's topped with hard-boiled eggs and serrano jamón (cured ham). During the scorching Andalusian summers, this refreshing dish is a favorite choice.

2. Rabo de Toro: Rabo de Toro is a soft and tasty oxtail stew popular in Cordoba. Oxtail is slow-cooked until it is meltingly soft and is frequently served with a rich, flavorful sauce.

3. Flamenqun: Flamenqun is a Cordoban meal produced by wrapping ham and cheese slices around a piece of meat, typically pork or chicken. The entire product is then breaded and deep-fried to crisp perfection.

4. Berza Cordobesa: Berza Cordobesa is a hearty and flavorful stew composed with chickpeas, pork, and cabbage. During the colder months, it's a popular comfort food.

5. Ajo Blanco: Ajo blanco is a chilled almond and garlic soup that is sometimes topped with grapes and served as a light snack.

6. Salmorejo Cordobés: This is a regional salmorejo with subtle differences in ingredients and flavors. It's popular because of its creamy texture and robust flavors.

7. Pastel Cordobés: A pastry filled with either a sweet or savory filling, such as sweet potato or spinach. It's a delectable dish appreciated by both locals and visitors.

8. Cordoban Wines: Cordoba is well-known for its wine production, particularly Montilla-Moriles wines. These fortified wines, comparable to sherry, are frequently consumed as an aperitif or with regional cuisine.

9. Tuna and fish: Because Cordoba is close to the ocean, fresh fish and tuna are common in its cuisine. Look for tuna dishes such as "mojama" (salt-cured tuna).

10. Tapas Culture: The tapas culture of Cordoba is dynamic and diversified. When you order a drink at a local tavern, you almost always get a free tapa. Discover the world of tapas, from traditional favorites like olives and cheese to more substantial and inventive meals.

Cordoba, like many other Andalusian cities, has a vibrant tapas culture. When you order a drink at a local tavern, you'll usually get a free tapa, which can range from olives and cheese to more substantial entrees.

It is crucial to appreciate local culinary traditions and discover the city's numerous tapas bars and restaurants when dining in Cordoba. Whether you stick to the classics or branch out, Cordoban food delivers a rich and gratifying experience that honors the city's cultural past. In the sections that follow, we'll take you to some of the best venues to eat Cordoban meals and tapas.

Trying these delicacies is not only a gourmet adventure, but also an opportunity to learn about Cordoba's rich culinary traditions. To sample these delectable Cordoban specialities, visit local restaurants, tapas bars, and traditional eateries.

Restaurants and Cafes in the Neighborhood

Cordoba has a thriving culinary scene, with a diverse selection of restaurants, tapas bars, and cafes where you can sample traditional Cordoban cuisine and soak up the local ambiance. Here are some local eateries and cafes to visit while you're here:

1. Salinas Taberna

Taberna Salinas is a classic Cordoban tavern famed for its superb tapas and welcoming atmosphere. It is located in the heart of the historic area.

Try their salmorejo, flamenqun, or any of their seasonal tapas. Pair your meal with a glass of local wine or a cool "rebujito" (sherry and soda cocktail).

2. The Churrasco

El Churrasco is a well-known restaurant that specializes on traditional Cordoban and Andalusian food. It's well-known for its grilled meats and friendly atmosphere.

Must-Try: Their rabo de toro (oxtail stew) and grilled meats, such as the "churrasco" (grilled steak), are not to be missed. Their wine list wonderfully complements the food.

3. Campos Estate Winery

Bodegas Campos is a historic restaurant housed in a 19th-century structure. It provides fine dining with a focus on Cordoban and Andalusian cuisine.

Must-Try: Their "salmorejo cordobés, " "flamenqun, " and traditional Cordoban stews are all must-tries. The wine cellar of the restaurant has a large selection of regional wines.

4. Pepe de la Judera's House

Casa Pepe de la Judera, located in the heart of the Jewish Quarter, provides a beautiful setting for feasting on Andalusian cuisine.

Try their berza cordobesa (chickpea and cabbage stew), ajo blanco, and other tapas. The courtyard of the restaurant is a beautiful spot to eat.

5. Auxiliary Taberna Sociedad Plateros Mara

This modest tapas bar provides a variety of conventional and unique tapas as well as a pleasant ambiance.

Try their ever-changing tapas menu, which includes regional delicacies as well as imaginative creations. Tapas should be paired with local wines or "cerveza. "

6. Correos Coffee Shop

Café de Correos is a traditional cafe located close to the Mezquita-Cathedral. It's a great place for coffee, pastries, and light dinners.

Try a cup of Cordoban coffee with a slice of classic pastry like "pastel cordobés. "

7. La Montillana Taberna

This welcoming bar specializes in Montilla-Moriles wines and serves a range of tapas to go with them.

Try their large wine collection, which includes local sherry-style wines. Pair your wine with one of their savory tapas, which frequently contain cured meats and cheeses.

8. Santos Café & Bar

Café Bar Santos is a local favorite noted for its coffee, breakfast menu, and laid-back attitude.

Start your day with a hearty Spanish breakfast of toast with tomato and olive oil, or treat yourself to a café con leche (coffee with milk) and a pastry.

These Cordoba restaurants and cafes offer a flavor of the city's culinary culture as well as a variety of eating experiences ranging from informal tapas outings to gourmet dining in historic settings. During your tour, be sure to take a look at the local cuisines and the many Cordoban dishes.

Cordoba Vegetarian and Vegan Options

Cordoba's culinary scene has expanded to accommodate a wide range of dietary needs, including vegetarian and vegan offerings. Here are some Cordoba restaurants and cafes that serve amazing vegetarian and vegan dishes:

1. Vegan Empanadas

El Empastre Vegano is a vegan restaurant located in Cordoba's old center. They serve vegan burgers, sandwiches, and salads, among other plant-based options.

Must-Try: Their vegan "salmorejo" and the "Empastre Burger, " which is a local favorite.

2. Bistró Bardulia Café

Bardulia Café Bistró is well-known for its vegetarian and vegan selections for breakfast, brunch, and lunch. It's a cozy cafe with a laid-back vibe.

Must-Try: Their vegan "tortilla" (Spanish omelette) and daily changing specialties are a must-try.

3. Garum

Garum is a Cordoba restaurant that serves both classic and new food, including vegetarian and vegan options.

Must-Try: Their vegan "berza" (chickpea and cabbage stew) and "ajo blanco" (chilled almond and garlic soup) are both delicious.

4. Teresa Al-Zagal

Tetera Al-Zagal is a beautiful tea establishment located in Cordoba's Jewish Quarter. While it is well-known for its tea, it also serves vegetarian and vegan Middle Eastern-inspired cuisine.

Must-Try: Pair a cup of mint tea with their veggie couscous and vegan desserts.

5. Santos Bar

Description: As previously said, Bar Santos is a local popular cafe that serves vegetarian and vegan brunch options. They sell delicacies like tomato toast with olive oil, which may be made vegan.

Start your day with their delectable vegetarian or vegan breakfast options combined with a cup of coffee.

6. La Montillana Taberna

While Taberna La Montillana is most renowned for its wines and tapas, it also serves vegetarian and vegan tapas.

Must-Try: Their seasonal vegetarian and vegan tapas, which frequently include dishes like roasted veggies and marinated olives, are a must-try.

These restaurants cater to vegetarians and vegans, ensuring that you can enjoy a variety of foods that correspond to your dietary needs while exploring Cordoba's gastronomic treasures. When dining at a local restaurant, make sure to ask about vegan alternatives or dietary adjustments, since many are ready to fulfill specific requests.

Cordoba Dining Etiquette

To have a nice and courteous meal experience in Cordoba, be informed of the local dining etiquette and customs. Here are some dining etiquette guidelines to remember:

1. Reservations: It's a good idea to make reservations, especially at popular restaurants, because Cordoba can get fairly crowded, especially during peak eating hours.

2. Tipping: is prevalent in Spain, and service personnel appreciate it. Depending on the level of service, it is customary to leave a tip of 10% to 15% of the cost. However, this is not required, and tipping is optional.

3. Seating: In most formal restaurants, the host or hostess will direct you to your table. Wait to be seated, and if you have a preference for where you'd like to sit, make it known nicely.

4. Table Manners: When dining in a formal environment, keep your hands on the table (but not your elbows) and place your napkin on your lap.

5. Bread and Olives: As a complimentary appetizer, restaurants typically serve a basket of bread and a small dish of olives. These are frequently not included in the bill, but it is courteous to inquire whether they are gratis or incur an additional price.

6. Ordering: When putting your order, be courteous and respectful to the server. Cordobans enjoy their meals slowly, there's no need to rush through your order. Requesting recommendations is also appropriate.

7. Sharing plates: It's customary in Cordoba's tapas culture to share plates with your dining mates. Feel free to order a variety of tapas to share with the party.

8. Wine and Alcohol: Spanish wine is well-known, and it is traditional to drink wine with your meal. If you don't drink wine, you can get water, soft drinks, or beer instead. If you order a bottle of wine and don't finish it, you can have it corked and taken with you.

9. Paying the Bill: When you're ready to pay the bill, make eye contact with the server or raise your hand slightly. Payment is normally paid in cash or by credit card, and it is common to wait for the server to process the payment at your table.

10. Rest time: Keep in mind that many Cordoba restaurants close for a siesta break in the afternoon, usually between 2:00 PM and

4:00 PM. If you want to eat during this time, be sure the establishment is open.

11. Courtesy: As with any eating experience, it's crucial to be kind and courteous to both the restaurant personnel and your fellow guests. Simple greetings and thankfulness expressions in Spanish, such as "por favor" (please) and "gracias" (thank you), go a long way.

You may completely enjoy your culinary experiences in Cordoba while respecting local customs and traditions if you follow these dining etiquette rules. Cordobans are famed for their great friendliness, and appreciating their culture and food will improve your overall eating experience in the city.

Chapter 6: Nightlife & Entertainment

Cordoba comes alive at night with a thriving nightlife scene that includes classic Spanish bars, boisterous pubs, and entertainment venues. In this chapter, we'll look at the top bars and pubs in Cordoba for a night out.

Pubs and Bars

Cordoba's bars and pubs are an important component of the city's nightlife, offering a unique opportunity to explore local culture, meet friendly residents, and sample a variety of drinks. Here are some of the best bars and pubs in Cordoba:

1. San Miguel Tavern

Taberna San Miguel is a delightful typical Andalusian tavern recognized for its welcoming environment and vast wine and beer choices. It's a terrific spot for tapas and regional delicacies.

2. La Montillana Taberna

This pub is well-known for its range of Montilla-Moriles wines and a variety of tapas to go with them. It's a favorite hangout for both residents and visitors.

3. Campos Estate Winery

Bodegas Campos is a renowned restaurant as well as a historic wine cellar where you may sample a wide choice of wines, including local Montilla-Moriles varietals. The atmosphere is ideal for a leisurely evening.

4. Salinas Taberna

Taberna Salinas is a classic Cordoban bar located in the old district. It is well-known for its delectable tapas and provides a quiet setting in which to experience regional delicacies.

5. Pepe de la Judera's House

Casa Pepe de la Judera, located in the Jewish Quarter, provides a pleasant environment for an evening out. They offer a wide range of beverages, including local wines and cocktails.

6. El Gallo Tapas

Taberna El Gallo is a prominent venue for live flamenco music. In an intimate atmosphere, sip a drink while watching skilled flamenco performers.

7. Hangar Sala Sala

Sala Hangar is a nightclub and live music venue where you may dance the night away to a variety of music genres. It's popular among the younger generation.

8. Correos Coffee Shop

Café de Correos is a traditional cafe located close to the Mezquita-Cathedral. It's a terrific spot to unwind with a cup of coffee, a cocktail, or a glass of wine.

9. Metrópolis Sala

Sala Metrópolis is a multipurpose venue that organizes a variety of events such as concerts, DJ sets, and themed parties. Check their calendar for forthcoming entertainment opportunities.

10. Paddy's Irish Pub and The Molly Malone are two Irish pubs in Cordoba where you can enjoy a pint of beer and a vibrant ambiance.

Keep in mind that the nightlife in Cordoba usually begins later in the evening, with many people going out about midnight. Cordoba has a diversified nightlife scene to suit all preferences, whether you prefer a peaceful evening at a traditional bar or dancing the night away at a nightclub.

Cordoba Live Music and Concerts

Cordoba has a vibrant music culture, with numerous venues holding live performances, concerts, and music events. Whether you enjoy classical music, flamenco, or modern music, there are entertainment alternatives to suit your musical preferences. Here are some live music and concert venues and events in Cordoba to consider:

1. Gran Teatro de Córdoba (Cordoba's Great Theater)

The Gran Teatro de Córdoba is a historic theatre that presents a variety of cultural events such as classical music concerts, opera, ballet, and theater productions. It is a legendary venue recognized for its majestic architecture and acoustics.

Check the theater's calendar for future classical concerts by local and international musicians.

2. El Gallo Tapas

This classic Cordoban bar is well-known not just for its beers and tapas, but also for its live flamenco performances. It provides an intimate space in which to enjoy true flamenco music and dancing.

Taberna El Gallo frequently hosts great local flamenco artists who demonstrate the heartfelt and passionate art genre.

3. Hangar Sala Sala

Sala Hangar is a nightclub and live music venue that presents a wide range of music events, such as concerts by local and traveling bands, DJ performances, and themed parties.

Events: Check out the Sala Hangar's event calendar for live music performances ranging from rock and pop to electronic and independent music.

4. Jardines de la Victoria (Victory Gardens)

Jardines de la Victoria is a beautiful park that occasionally hosts outdoor concerts and music festivals during the summer. It serves as a beautiful backdrop for live music concerts.

Events: Keep an eye out for periodic music festivals and open-air performances in this lovely garden setting.

5. Metrópolis Sala

Sala Metrópolis is a multi-purpose arena noted for holding a variety of events such as live music concerts, DJ nights, and themed parties. It is appealing to a variety of people.

Events: Check out their event calendar for events ranging from electronic dance music to alternative and rock artists.

6. Local Cafes and Bars

Many local taverns and cafes in Cordoba provide live music performances, especially during weekends. These smaller venues frequently showcase local bands and performers, creating an intimate and pleasant atmosphere.

Events: Speak with locals or look for posters and flyers in the city's pubs and cafés to learn about live music events taking place during your visit.

7. Peas Flamenco

Cordoba is well-known for its deep-rooted flamenco tradition. Look for "peas flamencas" (flamenco clubs) that host intimate flamenco performances on a regular basis. These events provide a one-of-a-kind and authentic glimpse into this Andalusian art form.

Check out the calendars of local flamenco peas for performances and events. They frequently showcase both established and rising artists.

Whether you prefer classical music, flamenco, or modern sounds, Cordoba's music scene allows you to immerse yourself in the city's rich cultural and musical legacy.

Cordoba's Theater and Performing Arts

Beyond music and dance, Cordoba's cultural landscape includes a variety of theater and performing arts activities. Cordoba has something for everyone, whether you like drama, comedy, or contemporary performances. Here are some theater and performing arts venues and events in the city to check out:

1. Gran Teatro de Córdoba (Cordoba's Great Theater)

The Gran Teatro de Córdoba is a famous and well-known theater in the city. It features a wide variety of performing arts events such as theater performances, ballet, opera, and classical music concerts.

Check the theater's calendar for future theatrical performances by local and touring theater companies. Dramas, comedies, musicals, and other performances are available in a lovely and historic setting.

2. Góngora Theatre

The Teatro Góngora is another well-known theater in Cordoba that is dedicated to supporting the performing arts. It presents a wide range of theatrical and cultural productions.

Events: Keep an eye on the program of Teatro Góngora for theatrical performances such as plays, dance performances, and cultural displays. It serves as a cultural center for the city.

3. The Axerqua Theatre

The Teatro Axerqua is an open-air theater located amid the picturesque Jardines de la Victoria. During the warmer months, it frequently holds outdoor acts such as theater, concerts, and cultural activities.

activities: Look for outdoor theater shows and cultural activities at Teatro Axerqua, which provides a one-of-a-kind experience in a beautiful garden environment.

4. Local Theater Organizations and Festivals

Cordoba boasts a thriving community of local theater organizations and artists that perform productions in various locations throughout the city on a regular basis. Throughout the year, the city also hosts theater festivals and events.

Events: Watch for news of theater performances by local and visiting troupes. Cordoba's theaters and cultural organizations frequently unite to provide audiences with a diverse range of theatrical experiences.

5. Festivals and street performances

Cordoba occasionally hosts street performances and theatrical festivals in public areas such as parks and squares. These events provide a more casual and approachable way to appreciate theater and performing arts.

Check the city's event calendars for details on street theater performances and festivals taking place during your visit. Local and international artists are frequently included at these events.

6. Cultural Institutions

Cordoba has various cultural centers, including the Casa de la Juventud and the Casa de las Tres Culturas, which host theater and performing arts performances, as well as workshops and cultural activities on occasion.

activities: Look through the cultural centers' programs to find theatrical performances, workshops, and cultural activities that interest you.

It's a good idea to check the schedules and ticket availability for theater and performing arts events in Cordoba ahead of time, especially for popular performances. Cordoba's cultural scene offers a varied assortment of options to participate with the performing arts, whether you're looking for classical theater, contemporary play, or outdoor performances.

Cordoba Nightclubs and Dancing

For those who enjoy dancing and staying out late, Cordoba's nightlife has a busy club scene. There are options for everyone to enjoy a night of dancing and entertainment, from modern clubs playing the newest tunes to locations with Latin, salsa, and flamenco moods. Here are some of Cordoba's best nightclubs and dancing spots:

1. Hangar Sala Sala

Sala Hangar is a well-known nightclub in Cordoba that conducts DJ nights and themed events with a variety of music genres ranging from electronic to pop to reggaeton and hip-hop.

Highlights include a lively environment, dance floors, and a wide range of music styles. Check out their events calendar for unique events and themed parties.

2. Metrópolis Sala

Sala Metrópolis is a multi-purpose arena that holds live music concerts, DJ performances, and themed parties. It caters to a varied audience and frequently includes electronic dance music and other genres.

Highlights: Enjoy a vibrant nightlife setting with a variety of music options. Keep an eye out for unique events and guest DJs.

3. The Irish Quarter Public House

The Irish Quarter Pub in Cordoba is a busy and pleasant bar where you can enjoy live music performances, including rock and pop bands, as well as DJ evenings.

Highlights: Dance to live music or sounds spun by DJs, and sample a variety of drinks in a comfortable setting.

4. Lounge La Bodeguita

La Bodeguita Lounge is a nightclub with a Latin and salsa vibe. It's a popular venue for Latin-inspired dancing and beverages.

Highlights: Practice your salsa, merengue, and bachata movements for an evening of dancing. The venue frequently hosts live Latin music and special events.

5. St. Anthony

El Sótano is a Cordoba underground nightclub notable for its eclectic music selection, which includes indie, alternative, and rock music. It's popular among the city's younger residents.

Highlights: This underground club with a focus on alternative and indie music offers a one-of-a-kind vibe.

6. Peas and Flamenco Clubs

Consider attending a flamenco club or "pea flamenca" for a new type of dancing experience, since these venues frequently offer live flamenco music and dance performances where you may enjoy traditional Andalusian dance and music.

Highlights: Immerse yourself in the passionate world of flamenco, with opportunity to see talented performers and even join in on the dancing if you're brave enough.

When visiting Cordoba's nightlife and dancing scene, take in mind that the nightlife typically begins late, with many locals leaving about midnight or later. Check the schedules of the venues for special events and parties, and make reservations if necessary for popular clubs and pubs. Cordoba has a vibrant nightlife that will provide night owls and dance aficionados with an interesting and memorable experience.

Chapter 7: Cordoba Shopping

Cordoba's shopping experience is fascinating, with a mix of traditional markets, boutique stores, and souvenir shops where you may buy unique presents and keepsakes to remember your visit. In this chapter, we'll look into shopping in Cordoba, with a focus on souvenirs and presents that represent the city's soul.

Souvenirs and Presents

When looking for souvenirs and gifts in Cordoba, you'll come across a wide range of things that reflect the city's rich culture, history, and customs. Consider the following popular souvenirs and gift ideas:

1. Hand-Painted pottery: Cordoba is famous for its hand-painted pottery. Decorative plates, tiles, and pottery with complex Moorish and Andalusian motifs are available. Look for pieces that depict the city's most recognizable sites, such as the Mezquita-Cathedral.

2. Spanish fans, known as "abanicos, " are not only useful for keeping cool but also make lovely keepsakes. They are available in a variety of forms, colors, and designs, and serve as a pleasant and portable memento of Cordoba.

3. Cordoba is well-known for its leather craftsmanship. Consider acquiring high-quality Spanish leather wallets, belts, bags, or accessories. Leather goods in the city are well-known for their quality and style.

4. Flamenco-Related Souvenirs: Cordoba is intimately associated with flamenco, and you can discover a variety of flamenco-related souvenirs, such as castanets, flamenco shawls, and posters of

famous flamenco musicians. These pieces encapsulate the spirit of Andalusian music and dancing.

5. Olive Oil and Products: Olive oil production is well-known in Andalusia. Bring home a bottle of Cordoba's quality extra virgin olive oil or investigate olive oil-based cosmetics, soaps, and gourmet goods.

6. Spanish Wine & Sherry: Because Cordoba is close to wine-producing regions, you may discover a variety of Spanish wines, including native Montilla-Moriles wines. Look for wine shops and ask about the best regional wines to bring home with you.

7. Discover one-of-a-kind handcrafted jewelry created by local craftsmen. Cordoba jewelry frequently incorporates Moorish-inspired designs and semi-precious stones.

8. Cordoban Guitar and Flamenco Accessories: If you enjoy music, try acquiring a Cordoban guitar or Flamenco accessories such as guitar picks and strings. Miniature guitars and beautiful flamenco accessories are also available.

9. Traditional Spanish costumes: Admire the craftsmanship of traditional Spanish costumes such as "flamenco dresses" and "trajes de gitana. " These dresses come in a variety of styles and make a lovely keepsake or gift for special occasions.

10. Alhambra Tiles: While Cordoba is famous for its Mezquita, you can also get Alhambra-inspired tiles in adjacent Granada. These colorful tiles are ideal for use as wall art or ornamental pieces in your home.

11. Local Art & Paintings: Look for paintings and artwork done by Cordoban artists in local art galleries and shops. You might come across pieces that capture the city's beauty and culture.

Remember to visit the city's markets, boutiques, and artisan shops when looking for souvenirs and gifts. You'll be able to support local artisans and bring home one-of-a-kind souvenirs that reflect the beauty and character of Cordoba.

Cordoba's Traditional Markets

Traditional markets in Cordoba offer a one-of-a-kind shopping experience where you can immerse yourself in local culture while discovering fresh food, artisanal products, and handcrafted handicrafts. These marketplaces are lively centres of activity, and studying them provides insights into city life. Here are several classic marketplaces in Cordoba that are worth a visit:

1. Victoria Marketplace

Mercado Victoria is a gourmet food market housed in a stunning nineteenth-century edifice. Locals and tourists alike go here to sample a range of Andalusian and foreign cuisines.

Highlights: Sample a variety of culinary pleasures, including tapas and shellfish, as well as pastries and international meals. It's a great spot to try regional specialties.

2. La Corredera Market

The Mercado de la Corredera is a bustling food and flea market in the lovely Plaza de la Corredera. It's a historic market with a lively atmosphere.

Highlights include fresh produce, local cheeses, cured meats, olives, and more. The flea market sector also sells antiques, crafts, and apparel.

3. La Victoria Market

The Mercado de la Victoria, popularly known as the Mercado de las Flores, is a bustling flower market. It's a colorful and fragrant location to visit close to the historic core.

Highlights: Take in the stunning array of flowers, plants, and floral creations. In the market area, you can also find handcrafted items and souvenirs.

4. The Santa Cruz Market

The Mercado de Santa Cruz is a lovely neighborhood market in the historic Jewish Quarter. It sells a wide range of fresh produce, meats, and local products.

Highlights: Shop for ingredients used in Cordoban and Andalusian cuisine in a traditional market atmosphere. It's a terrific spot to pick some regional delicacies.

5. The City of Children's Market

The Mercado de la Ciudad de los Nios is a family-friendly market in a park setting. It includes a variety of food kiosks as well as children's leisure activities.

Highlights: Enjoy a casual atmosphere with shopping and entertainment opportunities. Families can enjoy valuable time together in this wonderful location.

6. Córdoba Agricultural and Ganadero Market (MAGA)

MAGA is Cordoba's agricultural and animal market, where local farmers and producers congregate to offer their wares. It's a genuine market that offers insight into the region's agricultural history.

Highlights include a diverse selection of fresh and seasonal products such as fruits, vegetables, cheeses, and meats. It's a chance to support local farmers while also tasting the tastes of Cordoba.

When visiting Cordoba's traditional markets, keep in mind that hours of operation vary and that some markets may be closed on certain days. Exploring these markets allows you to meet the locals, enjoy regional flavors, and locate unique products that reflect the city's history and heritage.

Cordoba's High-End Boutiques

Cordoba has a number of high-end shops and designer stores where you can discover luxury fashion, accessories, and quality goods for those searching for a more affluent shopping experience. These boutiques appeal to sophisticated shoppers looking for unique and fashionable things. Here are some high-end boutiques to visit in Cordoba:

1. The Paseo de Gracia

Paseo de Gracia is a trendy shopping boulevard in Cordoba that is home to a number of high-end boutiques, designer retailers, and upmarket fashion companies.

Highlights include a look at well-known fashion companies and premium labels, as well as clothes, accessories, and footwear. It's an excellent choice for upmarket shopping in the city center.

2. The British Council

El Corte Inglés is a well-known Spanish department store with a presence in Cordoba. It sells a wide variety of high-quality items, including designer clothing, cosmetics, jewelry, and household goods.

Highlights: Shop the fashion departments for designer apparel, purses, and accessories from local and worldwide brands.

3. Cordoba, Zoco

Zoco Cordoba is a retail area that mixes high-end stores, artisan shops, and fine dining. It's a sophisticated retail location with a luxurious flair.

Highlights: Visit boutiques that sell prominent brands' apparel, jewelry, and accessories. After you've finished shopping, unwind at one of the center's elegant restaurants or cafes.

4. Mila Calzados

Calzados Mila is a well-known luxury shoe store in Cordoba, offering a carefully curated collection of high-quality footwear for men and women. They are well-known for their leatherwork.

Highlights: Browse a wide selection of exquisite and trendy shoes, including leather boots, dress shoes, and casual footwear.

5. López, Joyera

Joyera López is a prominent Cordoba jewelry store recognized for its superb variety of fine jewelry, watches, and luxury accessories.

Highlights: Browse through a gorgeous assortment of jewelry, including diamond and gemstone pieces, as well as luxury watches from well-known companies.

6. Designer Stores

Cordoba's central center is filled with trendy boutiques and high-end retail outlets. These shops feature the most recent collections from Spanish and international designers.

Highlights: Look for stores showcasing well-known designers, where you may get high-quality apparel, purses, shoes, and accessories.

7. Antique stores and art galleries

Cordoba also has art galleries and antique shops that offer discerning collectors unusual and high-end artwork, antiques, and collectibles.

Highlights: Visit these galleries and shops to find unique art, sculptures, vintage furniture, and decorative things.

While shopping in Cordoba's high-end stores, you'll be able to find exquisite apparel, accessories, and luxury items that reflect both contemporary and classic Spanish designs. Remember that operating hours and availability may vary, plan your shopping trips appropriately.

Cordoba's Shopping Districts

Cordoba has a number of shopping districts and neighborhoods with everything from traditional markets and artisan crafts to high-end boutiques and fashion retailers. Each shopping district has its own distinct personality and set of offerings. Here are some of Cordoba's main shopping districts:

1. Cruz Conde Avenue:

Calle Cruz Conde is one of Cordoba's principal shopping lanes, located in the city center. It's a thriving commercial district full of shops, boutiques, and department stores.

Highlights: Visit a variety of fashion boutiques, footwear stores, electronics stores, and other retailers. It's a fantastic location for both shopping and dining.

2. Victoria Boulevard:

Paseo de la Victoria is another popular shopping route in Cordoba, with a variety of fashion retailers, boutiques, and cafes. It's a bustling neighborhood full of shoppers and people.

Highlights: Shop for apparel and accessories at well-known brands as well as local businesses. Enjoy the bustling environment and stop in one of the many cafés for a coffee or a meal.

3. Calleja de las Flores (Flower Street):

Calleja de las Flores is a lovely passageway in Cordoba's ancient Jewish Quarter. While it is not a standard retail street, it is a wonderful spot to explore and find handcrafted items and souvenirs.

Highlights: Tucked away in this lovely alley are artisan stores, ceramics, jewelry, and local crafts. It's a terrific place to find unique keepsakes.

4. Cordoba, Zoco:

Zoco Cordoba is a modern commercial mall located near the Mezquita-Cathedral. It has a mix of high-end stores, artisan businesses, and restaurants.

Highlights: This modern shopping center contains upmarket fashion boutiques, artisan crafts, and speciality businesses. It's an ideal spot for both shopping and dining.

5. La Corredera Market:

Mercado de la Corredera is more than simply a conventional market; it's also a vibrant destination for shopping and socializing. It is situated in the lovely Plaza de la Corredera.

Highlights: Browse the market for fresh food, local products, antiques, and artisan crafts. It's a one-of-a-kind shopping experience in a historical atmosphere.

6. Gracia Boulevard:

Paseo de Gracia is a trendy shopping boulevard in Cordoba that is home to a number of high-end boutiques, designer retailers, and upmarket fashion companies.

Highlights include a look at well-known fashion companies and premium labels, as well as clothes, accessories, and footwear. It's an excellent choice for upmarket shopping in the city center.

7. Judera (Jewish Quarter):

Cordoba's ancient Jewish Quarter is a lovely neighborhood dotted with narrow alleyways, squares, and artisan shops. It's a charming spot for shopping and exploring.

Highlights: Explore the Jewish Quarter's picturesque streets for artisan crafts, jewelry, ceramics, and local products.

You'll find a wide choice of things in these Cordoba shopping districts, from fashion and accessories to artisan crafts and traditional goods. Take your time browsing, soak in the ambience, and discover one-of-a-kind gems that embody the essence of Cordoba's history and legacy.

Chapter 8: Day Trips & Excursions

For day trips and excursions, the surroundings of Cordoba provide a multitude of historical, cultural, and natural attractions. In this chapter, we'll look at some of the most interesting places to visit from Cordoba.

Azara Medina

Medina Azahara, widely known as the "Shining City, " is a UNESCO World Heritage Site located just outside of Cordoba. This archaeological complex bears witness to the splendor of the Umayyad Caliphate of Cordoba and offers an insight into the city's history.

Highlights

Palace Ruins: Explore the palace city's well-preserved ruins, which comprise majestic structures, courtyards, and arches that once displayed the Caliphate's luxury.

Visitor Center: Begin your journey with the modern visitor center, which features informative displays and audiovisual presentations about the site's history.

Panoramic Views: Enjoy panoramic views of the surrounding countryside and the city of Cordoba in the distance from various spots within Medina Azahara.

Learn about ongoing archaeological excavations and discoveries that are shedding light on the history of this once-magnificent metropolis.

Scenic Gardens: Take a stroll around the wonderfully maintained gardens that compliment the historical monument and provide a peaceful setting for introspection.

How to Get There: Medina Azahara is located about 8 kilometers (5 miles) west of Cordoba. It is accessible via automobile, cab, or guided trip.

A visit to Medina Azahara transports you to the Islamic period of Cordoba, allowing you to see the ruins of a city that once embodied the beauty of Al-Andalus.

Cordoba Sierra

The Sierra de Cordoba is a beautiful mountain range to the north of the city of Cordoba. This natural retreat provides a calm respite from city life, with chances for outdoor activities, picturesque drives, and discovery of attractive mountain communities.

Highlights

Natural Beauty: Take in the stunning natural beauty of the Sierra de Cordoba, which features lush forests, steep peaks, and pure rivers. Nature lovers and outdoor enthusiasts will adore it here.

Hiking & routes: Wander across the mountains' numerous hiking routes and walkways. Hiking in the Sierra de Cordoba allows you to find secret waterfalls, caverns, and panoramic perspectives.

Visit gorgeous communities like as Zuheros, Priego de Cordoba, and Almodovar del Rio, each with their own distinct charm, historic architecture, and local traditions. Don't pass up the opportunity to try regional food at a local eatery.

Discover the region's historical treasures, including ancient castles, churches, and monasteries that reflect the region's rich history. The Almodovar del Rio Castle, set on a hill, is a renowned attraction.

Bird Watching: The Sierra de Cordoba is a birdwatcher's paradise. Keep a look out for a variety of bird species in their native settings.

Beautiful Drives: Take beautiful drives over the hilly environment, with winding roads providing breathtaking vistas at every turn. Even the journey itself might be a memorable occasion.

Getting There: The Sierra de Cordoba is easily accessible by automobile from Cordoba. The drive takes about 1-2 hours, depending on where you want to go in the mountain range.

A day trip or excursion to the Sierra de Cordoba allows you to reconnect with nature, see attractive villages, and participate in outdoor activities in a tranquil and picturesque location. Whether you enjoy trekking, cultural exploration, or simply relaxing in a peaceful setting, the Sierra de Cordoba has something for everyone.

Montilla-Moriles Wine Tours

Montilla-Moriles is a well-known wine-producing region in Cordoba, well known for its fortified wines, particularly Montilla-Moriles sherry. Take a wine tour to learn about the region's vineyards, wineries, and the art of winemaking.

Highlights:

Winery Tours: Take a guided tour of a local winery to learn about the winemaking process, from grape cultivation to aging. Learn about the history and traditions of the Montilla-Moriles wines.

Tastings: Sample the region's distinctive wines, which may include Fino, Amontillado, and Pedro Ximenez sherry. Enjoy the rich flavors and aromas of these one-of-a-kind wines.

Vineyard Tours: Take a stroll through the gorgeous vineyards, where you can examine the grapevines and learn about the region's viticulture traditions.

Visit historical bodegas (wine cellars) that have been in operation for generations. Explore the atmospheric cellars and learn about the ancient winemaking procedures employed by Montilla-Moriles.

Local Cuisine: Many Montilla-Moriles wine trips incorporate food experiences. Enjoy food pairings with the wines, relishing Andalusian delicacies that pair wonderfully with the wines.

Wine tours frequently incorporate educational components, such as conversations about terroir, grape varietals, and the nuances of sherry production.

Bottling and Labeling: See how Montilla-Moriles wines are prepared for distribution by witnessing the bottling and labeling operations.

How to Get There: Montilla-Moriles is about 40 kilometers (25 miles) south of Cordoba. You can get to the region by car, taxi, or by joining one of the many organized wine excursions that include transportation.

A wine tour in Montilla-Moriles allows you to immerse yourself in the world of Spanish fortified wines, learn about the region's winemaking legacy, and sample some of Spain's greatest sherry wines. The trips include wine tasting, culinary pleasures, and cultural insights into the traditions of this ancient wine-producing region.

Carmona excursion

Carmona is a lovely hamlet located around 40 kilometers (25 miles) northeast of Cordoba. Carmona, known for its well-preserved medieval core, is a charming day excursion from Cordoba, providing a glimpse into Andalusia's rich cultural and architectural legacy.

Highlights:

Alcazar of Carmona: Begin your excursion in the Alcazar of Carmona, a beautiful fortification that dates back to Roman times and was later enlarged by the Moors. Explore its spectacular walls, towers, and courtyards while taking in the surrounding landscape.

Santa Maria de la Asuncion Church: Visit the Santa Maria de la Asuncion Church an outstanding example of Andalusian Gothic architecture. The inside of the church boasts elaborate altarpieces and a stunning Mudejar-style ceiling.

Roman Necropolis: Carmona is well-known for its Roman legacy, and you may see an ancient Roman necropolis with well-preserved tombs, such as the Roman Tomb of Servilia.

Old Town: Stroll through Carmona's picturesque streets, where you'll see whitewashed buildings, flower-filled balconies, and lovely squares. Don't miss the lovely Plaza de San Fernando.

Archaeological Museum: The Carmona Archaeological Museum houses a variety of items from the region's rich past, including Roman pottery and Moorish ceramics.

Gardens & Parks: Relax at Carmona's parks and gardens, such as the lush gardens of the Parador de Carmona and the Alcazar's lovely courtyard.

Local food: Sample Andalusian food at one of the region's restaurants or tapas bars. Carmona is well-known for its traditional meals, such as salmorejo (cold tomato soup) and succulent fish.

Getting There: Carmona is easily accessible by vehicle or public transit from Cordoba. The travel takes about 30-40 minutes, making it an ideal day vacation choice.

Carmona's rich history, gorgeous architecture, and peaceful atmosphere make it an ideal day excursion from Cordoba. Carmona provides a pleasant and culturally stimulating experience, whether you explore its old Roman sites, admire its Gothic architecture, or simply wander through its picturesque streets.

Surrounding Villages of Cordoba

Cordoba is surrounded by charming villages and towns, each with its own distinct personality, history, and attractions. Exploring these lovely communities provides an insight into rural Andalusian life as well as the chance to discover hidden jewels. Here are some nearby villages worth seeing:

1. Zuheros:

Zuheros, located south of Cordoba, is a lovely white town built on a slope overlooking olive groves. It is well-known for its magnificent castle, caves, and lovely medieval town.

Highlights include a visit to the Zuheros Castle, a visit to the famed Cueva de los Murciélagos (Bat Cave), and a stroll through the small lanes covered with flower-filled pots.

2. Cordoba Priego:

Priego de Cordoba is a charming village to the southeast of Cordoba known for its Baroque architecture, stunning fountains, and olive oil manufacturing.

Highlights include a visit to the Fuente del Rey, a group of magnificent fountains, a stroll around the old center with its Baroque buildings, and a tasting of local olive oil.

3. Del Rio, Almodovar:

Almodovar del Rio, located west of Cordoba, is famous for its magnificent castle, Castillo de Almodovar. On a hilltop above the village, the castle is located.

Highlights include a visit to the historical Castillo de Almodovar, exploration of the town's historic core, and panoramic views from the castle's towers.

4. Iznajar:

Iznajar, located south of Cordoba, is a lovely hamlet perched on a hill overlooking the enormous Iznajar Reservoir. It is well-known for its castle and charming old town.

Highlights include a visit to the Castillo de Iznajar, a stroll through the village's cobblestone alleys, and breathtaking views over the reservoir.

5. Baena:

Baena, located southeast of Cordoba, is a historic town with a long history of olive oil manufacturing. It is well-known for its stunning churches and convents.

Highlights include a walk around the town's ancient quarter, a visit to the Church of Santa Maria, and a visit to the Olive Oil Museum to learn about the olive oil industry.

6. Montoro:

Montoro, located along the Guadalquivir River north of Cordoba, is recognized for its scenic old town, ancient bridge, and traditional festivities.

Highlights include crossing the ancient Puente Romano (Roman Bridge), strolling around the picturesque streets, and attending local festivities like the Moros y Cristianos.

7. Bujalance:

Bujalance is a tiny village northeast of Cordoba recognized for its agricultural heritage, historic sites, and tranquil environment.

Highlights include a visit to the Church of San Francisco, exploration of the Plaza de Espaa, and enjoyment of the town's rural environment.

Each of these surrounding communities provides a distinct and authentic experience, showcasing the province's vast cultural and historical riches. Whether you want to visit historic monuments, enjoy the picturesque countryside, or sample local food, these villages provide a refreshing change of pace from the city and an opportunity to immerse yourself in Andalusian culture.

Chapter 9: Useful Information

We'll present crucial practical advice in this chapter to help you explore Cordoba successfully and make the most of your visit. Language and communication, transportation, currencies, and local customs will all be covered.

Communication and Language

Spanish is the official language of Cordoba and the larger Andalusian region. While many locals in Cordoba's tourist districts speak English, it's a good idea to learn a few basic Spanish phrases to make the most of your visit. Learning a few popular pleasantries, meal ordering words, and asking for directions might help make your stay more enjoyable.

Local Dialect: Andalusian Spanish has its own dialect and accent, which might deviate from standard Spanish at times. Be prepared to hear some variances in pronunciation and terminology.

Communication Pointers:

Learn some fundamental Spanish phrases like "hello" (hola), "please" (por favor), "thank you" (gracias), and "goodbye" (adiós).

When faced with language obstacles, consider using a translation software or phrasebook to help you communicate.

Politeness: In Spanish society, politeness is highly valued. It is appreciated to use "por favor" and "gracias" wherever suitable.

English-Speaking Services: In tourist destinations, English-speaking employees are more likely to be found at hotels, restaurants, and attractions. However, knowing some Spanish is always beneficial.

Be aware of the following emergency numbers: 112 (general emergency) and 091 (police).

Transport

Getting Around Cordoba: The historic city of Cordoba is compact and approachable, making it simple to explore on foot. However, for longer journeys or while visiting neighboring settlements, you have various options:

Cordoba has a public bus system that serves the city and its surrounding areas. Tickets are available for purchase on board or at kiosks. A train and bus terminal are also available for regional and long-distance travel.

Taxis are widely available in Cordoba. They can be flagged down on the street or found at taxi stops.

Renting a car can be a convenient alternative if you plan to visit the nearby areas or other cities. Just keep in mind that parking in the historic district might be difficult, and some areas may have restricted access.

Payment and Currency

The Euro (€) is the official currency in Cordoba.

ATMs (cajeros automáticos): ATMs are widely available around the city and allow you to withdraw cash. Most places, including hotels, restaurants, and stores, accept major credit and debit cards.

Tipping: is customary in Spain but not required as it is in some other nations. Although not necessary, it is customary to leave a gratuity of 5-10% of the bill in restaurants. Tipping taxi drivers and service personnel is appreciated but not required.

Regional Customs

Siesta: Cordoba, like many other Spanish cities, observes the siesta tradition. Many shops and companies may close for a few hours in the afternoon, usually between 2:00 and 5:00 PM. Plan your activities appropriately, and keep in mind that some services may be unavailable at this time.

Eating Schedule: Meal timings in Spain may differ from those in other nations. Lunch is usually served between 1:00 and 3:00 PM, while dinner is usually served later, around 8:00 PM. Some restaurants may not open for dinner until after 9:00 p. m.

While Cordoba has a reasonably relaxed dress code, you may want to dress modestly when visiting religious places such as the Mezquita-Cathedral. It's also a good idea to have comfortable walking shoes when visiting the historic district.

Local Festivals: Find out whether there are any local festivals or holidays taking place during your visit. Festivals are a terrific opportunity to learn about the local culture, but they can also disrupt company hours and availability.

Understanding these practical aspects of life in Cordoba can help you navigate the city with comfort and respect for local customs, enhancing your visit and enriching it culturally.

Safety Recommendations

Cordoba, like many other towns in Spain, is usually regarded as safe for visitors. However, taking steps to guarantee your safety and well-being while visiting the city is always recommended. Here are some precautions to take:

Be aware: Keep an eye on your surroundings, especially in crowded areas and tourist attractions. Keep a close check on your stuff and be wary of pickpockets.

Use Secure Bags: To discourage theft, carry a crossbody or anti-theft bag. When in a crowded environment, keep your bag zipped and in front of you.

Avoid Late-Night Solo Walks: While Cordoba is typically safe, it's best to avoid strolling alone late at night in poorly lighted or secluded locations. Stick to well-known routes.

Emergency Contacts: Learn the local emergency phone numbers, such as 112 for general emergencies and 091 for police.

Hotel Security: Use hotel safes to keep valuables such as passports, cash, and electronics. When you're not in your hotel room, make sure it's securely locked.

Local Scams: Be wary of popular tourist scams, such as distraction tactics or unsolicited help. Proceed on your way after politely declining.

Water Safety: Tap water in Cordoba is generally safe to drink, however bottled water is an option if you are concerned.

Traffic safety: Use authorized crosswalks and heed traffic signals when crossing streets. Keep an eye out for traffic, including bicycles and scooters.

Sun protection: Cordoba may get very hot in the summer. Wear sunscreen, a hat, and remain hydrated to protect yourself from the sun.

Medical and Health Services

Cordoba has medical facilities and services to meet the health needs of visitors. Here are some vital health and medical advice:

Travel Insurance: Consider getting travel insurance that covers medical emergencies, such as hospital stays and medical evacuations, before your trip.

Pharmacies: Pharmacies (farmacias) are widely available in Cordoba and are denoted with a green cross. They typically operate during regular work hours, but some pharmacies offer rotating 24-hour emergency service.

Healthcare Facilities: Cordoba has a number of hospitals and medical centers, both public and private. One of the city's main hospitals is Hospital Universitario Reina Sofia.

Prescription Medications: If you need prescription medications, bring plenty of them along with the relevant documents.

In the event of a medical emergency, phone 112 for assistance. This number can link you to emergency medical services, fire department, or police department.

vaccines: Before traveling to Cordoba, consult your healthcare physician or the World Health Organization (WHO) about any required vaccines.

Food and Water: While tap water in Cordoba is generally safe to drink, you may opt to consume bottled water. When eating at street food booths, be vigilant and make sure the food is properly cooked and served hot.

Consultations with a Pharmacist: If you have minor health concerns, you can seek advice and over-the-counter drugs from a pharmacist (farmacéutico).

By following these safety and health rules, you can have peace of mind during your visit to Cordoba and safeguard your well-being throughout your stay.

Chapter 10: Trip Planning

Suggestions for Itineraries

A journey to Cordoba may be a thrilling excursion that includes historical exploration, cultural immersion, and culinary delights. We give itinerary suggestions in this chapter to help you make the most of your visit to this wonderful city. These itineraries are designed to accommodate a variety of interests as well as the amount of time you have available.

One-Day Itinerary: Cordoba Highlights

Even if you only have one day in Cordoba, you can visit its most famous attractions:

Morning:

Mezquita-Cathedral: Begin your day with a visit to Cordoba's most famous landmark, the Mezquita-Cathedral. Discover its fascinating architecture and history.

Lunch:

Meal in the Jewish Quarter: Visit one of the exquisite eateries in the Jewish Quarter for a classic Andalusian meal. Try salmorejo or flamenqun, two local dishes.

Afternoon after Lunch

Visit the Alcazar de los Reyes Cristianos, a historic palace with lovely gardens and Roman mosaics. Take your time exploring the fortifications and admiring the vistas.

The Roman Bridge and the Guadalquivir River: Take a stroll along the Roman Bridge and take in the scenery of the river and the Mezquita-Cathedral.

Evening:

Patios of Cordoba (in season): If visiting during the Patio Festival season (typically in May), spend an evening exploring some of the city's wonderfully decorated patios.

Dinner in a typical Tavern: In a typical tavern, savor Andalusian tapas and wine. Try rabo de toro (bull's tail stew), a local specialty.

Itinerary for Two Days: Deeper Exploration

You may learn more about Cordoba's history and culture in just two days:

Day 1 (Just like in the One-Day Itinerary):

The morning and lunch activities from the one-day program should be followed.

Afternoon:

1. The historic Synagogue of Cordoba: one of Spain's few intact medieval synagogues, is worth a visit.

2. Calleja de las Flores: Take a stroll down the lovely Calleja de las Flores, a picturesque alley lined with flowers and brightly colored buildings.

Evening:

3. Flamenco Show: Attend a traditional flamenco performance at one of Cordoba's tablaos or cultural centers. This classic Andalusian art form is not to be missed.

Day 2:

Morning:

4. Medina Azahara: Begin your second day with a trip to the nearby archaeological site of Medina Azahara. Explore the old palace city's ruins.

Lunch:

5. Lunch at a Local Restaurant: Return to Cordoba for a delectable lunch at a local restaurant, where you may sample more Andalusian dishes.

Afternoon:

6. Artisan Craft Shopping: Spend the afternoon touring the artisan craft shops and markets of Cordoba. Look for leather products, ceramics, and other unique items.

Evening:

7. Evening Riverside Walk: Take a leisurely evening stroll along the Guadalquivir River, taking in the lit vistas of the Mezquita-Cathedral.

Dinner at a Riverfront Restaurant: Savor the local cuisine while taking in the ambiance by dining at a riverfront restaurant.

Itinerary for Three Days: Leisurely Exploration

With three days in Cordoba, you may slowly tour the city and perhaps go on a day trip:

Day 1 and Day 2 (Same as in the Two-Day Itinerary):

Follow the two-day itinerary's activities.

Day 3 (Day Trip to an Adjacent Village):

Select a Village: For a day trip, choose one of the adjacent communities described in Chapter 8 (for example, Carmona, Zuheros, or Iznajar).

Spend the day seeing the village's historic sites, eating local cuisine, and immersing yourself in local culture.

Return to Cordoba: In the evening, return to Cordoba to relax and dine at your leisure.

These itineraries combine Cordoba's historical, cultural, and natural features, providing a memorable and enriching visit to this enchanting city. Plan your visit around your interests and take in all that Cordoba has to offer.

Packing Suggestions for a Trip to Cordoba

Packing for your vacation to Cordoba involves some thought, since the weather, cultural norms, and planned activities will all influence what you need to carry. Here are some packing suggestions to help you prepare for your trip to this lovely city:

1. Weather-Responsive Clothing:

Lightweight and breathable apparel: Because Cordoba has scorching summers, lightweight, breathable clothing is needed. Pack easy-to-wear shirts, shorts, skirts, and dresses. To protect yourself from the sun, wear a wide-brimmed hat and sunglasses.

Layering Options: If you're visiting in the spring or fall, bring layers. Nights can be cold, so bring a lightweight coat or sweater.

Clothing should be modest: When visiting religious or cultural buildings like as the Mezquita-Cathedral, it is important to dress modestly. Covering your shoulders and knees is required. Carry a scarf or shawl with you that you can easily drape over your shoulders if necessary.

2. Footwear that is comfortable:

Walking Shoes: The old heart of Cordoba is best visited on foot. For sightseeing and exploring, wear comfortable, supportive walking shoes or sandals.

3. Travel Accoutrements:

A tiny daypack or crossbody bag: is excellent for carrying essentials such as a water bottle, sunscreen, a map, and your camera.

Power Bank: Use a portable power bank to keep your electronic gadgets charged, especially if you rely on your phone for navigation.

Adapters: Type C and Type F power outlets are used in Spain. Bring the proper travel adaptor with you to charge your devices.

4. Toiletries and pharmaceuticals:

Travel-Sized Toiletries: Bring travel-sized toiletries with you or buy them when you arrive. If necessary, most toiletries can be found in local stores.

Prescription Medications: If you take prescription medications, bring plenty of them with you, as well as a copy of your prescription.

5. Travel documentation:

Passport and Visa: Make sure your passport is current, and verify the visa requirements for Spain based on your nationality.

Carry a copy of your travel insurance policy and contact details with you.

Make printed copies of vital documents (passport, insurance, itinerary) and securely save digital copies.

6 Finances & Money:

Cards: Bring at least one major credit card and one debit card for ATM withdrawals. To avoid card complications, notify your bank of your vacation plans.

Cash: While credit cards are generally accepted, having some cash (Euros) on hand for little transactions and establishments that do not accept cards is a good idea.

7 Sun Defense:

Sunscreen: Cordoba, especially in the summer, may be very sunny. A high SPF sunscreen should be brought for skin protection.

Sunhat and sunglasses: Use a sunhat and sunglasses to shield your eyes and face from the sun.

9 Items of Convenience:

Travel Pillow: If you are traveling to Cordoba for an extended period of time, a travel pillow can make your journey more comfortable.

10. Travel Health Prerequisites:

First aid kit: Carry a basic first-aid kit containing essentials such as band-aids, pain killers, and other drugs you may require.

Insect Repellent: Depending on the season and your planned activities, you may need insect repellent.

11. Recreation:

Bring books, e-readers, or travel games for amusement throughout your trip.

You may make your trip to Cordoba more comfortable, pleasurable, and memorable by packing intelligently and considering the local climate and culture. Before packing, double-check any special requirements or advice from your accommodation or tour providers.

Budgeting and Costs for Your Cordoba Trip

Budgeting for your vacation to Cordoba entails budgeting for a variety of expenses like as lodging, meals, transportation, activities, and incidentals. Here's a breakdown of prospective prices and budgeting advice:

1. Arrangements:

Budget Hotels and Hostels: Cordoba has affordable hostels and budget hotels for budget tourists. Prices vary, but you should budget between €20 and €60 each night.

Mid-Range Hotels: These hotels provide additional comfort and amenities. Prices per night normally range from €70 to €150.

Luxury Hotels: Luxury hotels and boutique lodgings can range in price from €150 to €300 per night or more.

Tip: To save money on lodging, try reserving ahead of time and looking for bargains and discounts. Staying in the city center is handy, but it may be more expensive than options slightly outside of the center.

2. Dining and Food:

Street Food and Local Cafes: Street food and local cafes provide inexpensive dining options. A lunch can be had for as little as €5 to €10.

Mid-Range Restaurants: A three-course meal at a mid-range restaurant may cost between €15 and €30 per person.

Fine Dining: Prices for fine dining places and luxury restaurants can range from €50 to €100 or more per person.

Try local tapas bars for inexpensive and tasty little plates. For lunch, it's also typical to offer a "menu del da," which often comprises many courses at a fixed price.

3. Modes of transportation:

Public Transportation: The public transportation system in Cordoba is quite efficient. A single bus ticket costs approximately €1.30, and a taxi fare begins at €3.50.

Car Rentals: Renting a car might make it easier to explore the nearby areas. Prices vary depending on the type of vehicle and the length of the rental.

Consider getting a transportation pass or card if you want to utilize public transportation frequently.

4. Activities and Sightseeing:

Fees for sights such as the Mezquita-Cathedral and the Alcazar de los Reyes Cristianos range from €5 to €12.

Guided Tours: Prices for guided tours vary depending on the type and duration of the tour.

Tip: Some attractions provide free admission at certain seasons of the year, so look for any deals or discounts.

5. Unexpected Expenses:

Shopping: Set aside money for souvenirs and shopping. Cordoba has many businesses that sell artisan crafts and local items.

While tipping is not required, it is usual to offer a small tip at restaurants and for service employees if the service was exceptional.

Have some emergency savings saved up for unexpected bills or crises.

For payment flexibility, keep a combination of cash and credit/debit cards on hand.

6. travel insurance:

Travel Insurance: Don't forget to account for the expense of travel insurance. Travel insurance costs vary according to coverage and duration.

7. Foreign Exchange:

Currency Exchange: Be aware of currency exchange rates and any costs that may be incurred when exchanging currency or withdrawing cash from an ATM.

To obtain the greatest bargain, examine conversion rates and consider using ATMs to get cash in the local currency.

8. Budgeting Suggestions:

Plan: Make a precise budget before your trip to ensure you have enough money to cover all expected expenses.

Pay in Local Currency: Pay in Euros wherever possible to avoid unfavorable exchange rates

Stay in Low-Cost Accommodations: If you intend to spend the majority of your time touring the city, consider staying in low-cost accommodations.

Eat Like a Local: Try local cuisine at reasonable prices, as well as street food and tapas.

Use Public transit: When navigating the city, choose cost-effective public transit options.

Pre-book Activities: To take advantage of any available discounts, consider pre-booking activities and attractions online.

You may have a great and pleasurable trip to Cordoba without splurging if you plan and manage your budget correctly. Keep track of your spending when traveling to ensure that you stay within your budget.

Conclusion

As we close the book on this Cordoba Travel Guide, we hope you're well-prepared and excited to go on your journey to this interesting city in the heart of Andalusia. Cordoba, with its centuries of history, peaceful blend of cultures, and breathtaking architectural marvels, provides an unforgettable vacation experience.

You've dug into Cordoba's vivid tapestry of past and present across the pages of this guide. You've seen the magnificent Mezquita-Cathedral, walked through the Jewish Quarter's tiny streets, experienced the flavors of Cordoban food, and discovered the tranquillity of its patios. You've learned about the city's history, practical information for planning your vacation, and ethical travel practices to ensure a good impact on the city and its inhabitants.

Cordoba is a city where time seems to stand still, where the legacy of its varied cultural influences can be seen in every stone, and where the past reverberates through its historic landmarks. It's a place to relish life's simple pleasures, like a leisurely stroll along the Guadalquivir River, a moment of introspection in the grounds of the Alcazar, or the thrill of eating tapas with newfound friends.

But keep in mind that your adventure in Cordoba isn't restricted to these pages; it's a unique voyage waiting to be told. Soak up the environment, immerse yourself in the culture, and let the city's allure bloom in front of you. Cordoba has a way of leaving an indelible stamp on your heart as you explore its streets and interact with its people.

As you enter Cordoba, take in the city's warmth, history, and vibrant soul. Your Cordoba adventure is about to begin, full of amazement, connection, and discovery. So pack your bags, put on your comfortable shoes, and head out to discover Cordoba's wonders.

May your travels be filled with unique experiences, important encounters, and life-long memories. Safe travels, and may your Cordoba journey exceed your expectations. Hasta luego! (I'll see you soon!)

Printed in Great Britain
by Amazon